LIVE LENT
at Home

Daily Prayers and Activities
FOR FAMILIES

Paige Byrne Shortal

Liguori
ONE LIGUORI DRIVE
LIGUORI MO 63057-9999

Imprimi Potest:
Thomas D. Picton, C.Ss.R.
Provincial, Denver Province
The Redemptorists

Published by Liguori Publications
Liguori, Missouri

To order, call 800-325-9521
www.liguori.org

Library of Congress Cataloging-in-Publication Data

Shortal, Paige Byrne.
 Live Lent at home : daily prayers and activities for families / Paige Byrne Shortal.—1st ed.
  p. cm.
 ISBN 978-0-7648-1869-1
 1. Lent—Prayers and devotions. 2. Families—Religious life. I. Title.
 BV85.S53 2010
 242'.34—dc22

2009052351

Liguori Publications, a nonprofit corporation, is an apostolate of the Redemptorists. To learn more about the Redemptorists, visit Redemptorists.com.

Interior photos: DesignPics, ShutterStock

Printed in the United States of America
14 13 12 11 10   5 4 3 2 1
First edition

Puzzle Solutions

Page 12–Map Locations: 1. 40 days; 2. Moses and Elijah; 3. A woman–we don't know her name; 4. Jerusalem; 5. Lazarus; 6. "Hosanna!"–a shout of acclamation or praise, from the Hebrew meaning "pray, save us!" 7. His disciples; 8. Calvary or Golgotha, outside the walls of Jerusalem; 9. Tomb–a place, usually carved into rock, where the dead were buried. Jesus' tomb was found empty because he was raised by God the Father to new life. • Page 27–Cryptogram: Words to Live By: "One does not live by bread alone, but by every word that comes from the mouth of God." • Page 37–Hidden Message: Are You Listening? "This is my Son, the beloved; listen to Him!" • Page 47–Crossword: Thirsty for God: 1. Jacob; 2. bucket; 3. well; 4. (Across) testimony; (Down) thirsty; 5. Jerusalem; 6. Messiah; 7. disciples; 8. Joseph; 9. worship; 10. prophet; 11. Christ; 12. salvation; 13. journey; 14. ancestors; 15. Samaria; 16. water • Page 67–Word Hook-Up: Test Your Lent Knowledge: 1. D, 2. F, 3. J, 4. E, 5. H 6. C, 7. K, 8. B, 9. G, 10. L, 11. A, 12. I • Page 77–Scrambled Words or Scrambled Eggs: 1. Easter; 2. egg; 3. chocolate; 4. jellybeans; 5. bunny; 6. basket; 7. bonnet; 8. Jesus; 9. hunt; 10. Alleluia; 11. lily; 12. risen.

LESHO

Table of Contents

Puzzle Solutions	2
Note to the Grownups	4
Note to the Kids	5
Lent Begins	**7**
Ash Wednesday Gospel	7
Weekday Reflections & Activities	8
Prayer: Sign of the Cross	11
Fun Page: Map to a Happy Easter	12
Stations of the Cross	14
First Week of Lent	**19**
Sunday Gospel	19
Weekday Reflections & Activities	20
Prayer: Our Father	26
Fun Page: Cryptogram	27
Second Week of Lent	**29**
Sunday Gospel	29
Weekday Reflections & Activities	30
Prayer: Glory Be	36
Fun Page: Hidden Message	37
Third Week of Lent	**38**
Sunday Gospel	38
Weekday Reflections & Activities	40
Prayer: Act of Contrition	46
Fun Page: Crossword	47

Fourth Week of Lent	**48**
Sunday Gospel	48
Weekday Reflections & Activities	50
Prayer: Hail Mary	56
Fun Page: Hidden Objects	57
Fifth Week of Lent	**58**
Sunday Gospel	58
Weekday Reflections & Activities	60
Prayer to Our Guardian Angel	66
Fun Page: Word Hook-up	67
Holy Week	**68**
Gospels of Holy Week	68
Holy Week Reflections & Activities	69
Prayer: Apostles' Creed	76
Fun Page: Scrambled Words	77
Easter Sunday	**78**
Gospel for Easter Sunday	78
Prayer: Come Holy Spirit	79
Fun Page: Color by Number	80

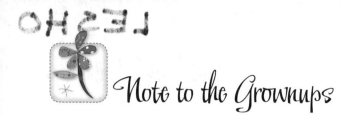

Note to the Grownups

Dear Mom, Dad, Grandparent, Uncle, Aunt,
Godparent, or Caring Adult:

This little book is for you and the children in your life. I remember when my sons were young and how difficult it was sometimes to pay attention at Mass. Now that I have young grandchildren, I'm reminded all over again. That's why in this book the Sunday Gospels for Lent are reprinted, followed by a daily reflection on the Gospel message, a discussion question or sometimes a suggested activity, and always a prayer to say together with your family. Each week there's also a traditional prayer to teach your children and an activity page. (Those were fun to prepare—hope you enjoy them.)

As I wrote this book, I remembered chaotic school nights and trying to fit in soccer practice, scout meetings, homework—not to mention a decent meal and a bath. Finding time to pray together wasn't always easy. We did say grace before each meal (holding hands so the youngest wouldn't dive into the food), and sometimes we would substitute a seasonal prayer for the usual "Bless us, O Lord…." Bedtime was when we read to our children and said simple night prayers. Car time was when we had our most significant discussions. The early morning was when I did my spiritual reading and writing.

Routine is especially important to children. They are little people in a huge, complex world, and routine gives them a sense of security and order. One son's morning greeting was always, "What's the plan?" Now that's his little daughter's morning greeting, too: "What's the plan?"

This book provides a plan for Lent. It's designed to be consulted every day. If you miss a day here and there, come back to it. Ask Jesus to help you and your family observe Lent so that you're ready for a glorious Easter. That's the plan!

Blessed Lent to you and yours,

Paige

Note to the Kids

Dear Kids:

Let me tell you something right away: I was never a Catholic kid. I didn't discover the Church until I was a grownup, so I don't know what it's like to be you. When my three sons were young, they found Lent kind of exciting, at least at the beginning, and kind of a drag, especially in the middle. But if they could make it all the way to the end, still keeping their Lenten promises—well, then they felt pretty special. Now I get to watch my grandchildren discover Lent and Easter.

This little book is to help you and your family make a good Lent together. The first few days will help you decide what you want to do for Lent—what you might give up or what extra thing you might do.

Whatever you decide to do for your "Lenten discipline," remember to ask Jesus to help you keep your promises and thank him for all that he promised us. I hope this little book helps you make a good Lent and that, when Easter finally comes six weeks from now, you feel really special because…you are!

God bless you,
Nana Paige

Lent Begins

ASH WEDNESDAY GOSPEL: MATTHEW 6:1–6, 16–18

"Beware of practicing your piety before others in order to be seen by them; for then you have no reward from your Father in heaven.

"So whenever you give alms, do not sound a trumpet before you, as the hypocrites do in the synagogues and in the streets, so that they may be praised by others. Truly I tell you, they have received their reward. But when you give alms, do not let your left hand know what your right hand is doing, so that your alms may be done in secret; and your Father who sees in secret will reward you.

"And whenever you pray, do not be like the hypocrites; for they love to stand and pray in the synagogues and at the street corners, so that they may be seen by others. Truly I tell you, they have received their reward. But whenever you pray, go into your room and shut the door and pray to your Father who is in secret; and your Father who sees in secret will reward you.

"And whenever you fast, do not look dismal, like the hypocrites, for they disfigure their faces so as to show others that they are fasting. Truly I tell you, they have received their reward. But when you fast, put oil on your head and wash your face, so that your fasting may be seen not by others but by your Father who is in secret; and your Father who sees in secret will reward you."

Ash Wednesday

To think about...

Funny thing about today—even though Ash Wednesday is not a holy day of obligation, the church is always crowded. One pastor used to joke that it's because the church is giving away something for free (ashes), but surely that can't be it. Yet even "casual Catholics" connect with this sign of ashes. We walk through the day with dirty faces, admitting to the world that we are not perfect, that there is room for change, that we long for a deeper relationship with God.

Catholics are obliged to fast today. This means that we don't eat meat and we eat sparingly—two small meals that are enough to sustain us but don't fill us up, one regular meal, and nothing in between meals. Note: These rules don't apply to children, the elderly, and pregnant or nursing women, but it's a good idea to instill this habit in children without endangering their health.

To do and to talk about...

Go to Mass today and receive the sign of ashes. Notice that the altar cloth is purple—the color the Church uses during penitential seasons. Carefully read the Gospel for today and identify the three elements of observing Lent: giving to the poor (alms), fasting, and prayer. The Lenten season actually begins this Sunday. Today is the beginning of the Lenten fast, so we are given a kind of warm-up period—several days to figure out how we want to observe Lent. Talk today about what you want to give up or add to your family's daily routine.

Let us pray...

Lord Jesus, bless us as we begin this
journey of Lent with you so that on Easter
we may feel you rising within us.
We pray, Lord, let us be like you.
Amen.

Thursday after Ash Wednesday

To think about...

Almsgiving, fasting and prayer—these are the three elements of Lent. Isn't it interesting that most religions encourage these three practices during their penitential seasons? Christians of many denominations, Jews and Muslims, Hindus and Buddhists—all observe a period of sacrifice and attention to the spiritual.

Why does Lent include charity to the poor? Perhaps it's because our relationship with God is never just two-way, but always includes others, especially those most in need. Jesus was adamant about this. In the Parable of the Sheep and the Goats (Matthew 25:31–46), Jesus tells us that what we do for others we do for him, and that when we neglect others, we are neglecting him. This is the only place in the Gospels where Jesus tells us what we need to do to get into heaven. Hmmm...maybe we'd better listen.

To do and to talk about...

Create an alms vessel today. It may be a little box or a jar or a tin can that your children can decorate, with liberal use of their purple crayon! Put it in a place where you will see it and be reminded to put something in it every day. Ask God's blessing on your alms vessel.

Let us pray...

Lord Jesus,
bless our alms vessel today.
Let it be a sign of your love
and your desire for us to love each other as you love us.
And, Jesus, please bless the poor,
especially those who have no one to pray for them.
We pray, Lord, let us be like you.
Amen.

Friday after Ash Wednesday

To think about...

"What are you giving up for Lent?" I love to listen to children talk about what they're giving up. One of my sons would present a long list of his intended sacrifices—which would maybe last until Ash Wednesday afternoon. His younger brother was less demanding of himself. He would announce that he was giving up mayonnaise, which he hated, or steak, which we never ate. One year I gave up rushing. I was in full-time ministry, a graduate student, and the mother of three young kids. I was always rushing, even when there was no place I had to be. It had become a habit. I gave up rushing, and it was liberating, not only for that Lent, but even now—twenty years later. Some folks fast from television or electronic games or chatting online—whatever threatens to take you away from your immediate duties and attention to those you love. And, of course, many choose to give up a favorite food. Sometimes it's the seemingly trivial sacrifice that is the hardest for the long haul. There is that voice within us saying, "Oh, come on, what harm can one piece of chocolate do?"

To do and to talk about...

Decide today how you will fast, pray, and give alms during Lent. Talk about it with your family and let each member write down their intentions on a slip of paper. Then place your paper in the alms vessel with a prayer.

Let us pray...

Lord Jesus,
today we promise to share our blessings with the poor,
to fast so that we might remember your sacrifice,
and to talk to you—to pray. Give us the grace to keep
our Lenten promises. We pray, Lord, let us be like you.
Amen.

Sign of the Cross

The third element of Lent, in addition to almsgiving and fasting, is prayer. We can pray alone and with our families and, of course, with our church community. Lent is a good time to begin a habit of prayer.

The Sign of the Cross is the most basic Christian prayer. It is a prayer of blessing, a prayer of dedication of ourselves to God, and a prayer of faith in the power and love of Jesus for us. Teach your children how to make the Sign of the Cross and encourage them to do so whenever you pray.

Typically we use the right hand, although if there is need, the left may be used. First touch the forehead and say, "In the name of the Father"; then touch the breast above the heart and say, "and of the Son"; then the left shoulder and say, "and of the Holy"; and finally the right shoulder while saying, "Spirit. Amen."

The sign of the cross may also be made with the thumb or forefinger on your child's forehead before they go to sleep at night or when you greet them in the morning or before they leave the house for school. It is the parents' privilege to bless their children, asking God to keep them safe and well and on the right path.

Many homes have a small font or container of holy water inside the door just as we do in church. When we dip our fingers into the holy water and sign ourselves with the cross, this reminds us that we are baptized Christians and committed disciples of Jesus.

Fun Page

Map to a Happy Easter!

Lent is a kind of journey with stops along the way. When you start out on a journey, it's a good idea to have a map. Follow Jesus on this journey through Lent to Easter.

First Sunday of Lent

Desert—Jesus retreats to the desert for forty days to prepare for his journey.

Second Sunday of Lent

Mountain—Jesus is transfigured and talks with Elijah and Moses.

Third Sunday of Lent

Samaria—Jesus accepts a drink from a woman at a well and offers her new life.

Fourth Sunday of Lent

On a road in Jerusalem—Jesus heals the young man born blind.

Easter Sunday
Empty tomb—Jesus is Risen! Alleluia!

Good Friday
Calvary or Golgotha, outside the walls of Jerusalem—Jesus dies on the cross for us.

Holy Thursday
Upper Room in Jerusalem—Jesus celebrates his Last Supper with his disciples and washes their feet.

Palm Sunday
Streets of Jerusalem—Jesus rides through the streets on a donkey to the shouts of "Hosanna!"

Fifth Sunday of Lent
Martha and Mary's house in Bethany—Jesus raises Martha and Mary's brother, Lazarus, from the dead.

Test your Map Knowledge

1. How long did Jesus stay in the desert?
2. Who did Jesus talk with on the mountain while he was transfigured?
3. Who gave Jesus a drink in Samaria?
4. In what town did Jesus heal the man who was born blind?
5. Who was Mary's and Martha's brother?
6. What did the people shout as Jesus rode a donkey?
7. Whose feet did Jesus wash?
8. Where did Jesus die on the cross?
9. What is a tomb? Why is it important that Jesus' tomb was found empty?

Answers on page 2

Stations of the Cross

Introduction

This is an ancient devotion, yet it always seems new because it is about our personal journey with Jesus. You can pray this devotion in church while walking from station to station or at home. Maybe the children will want to make their own booklet of pictures, one for each station.

Pray after the announcement of each Station ❀

Leader We adore you, O Christ and we bless you.

All   **Because by your Holy Cross you have redeemed the world.**

First Station: Jesus is condemned to death. ❀

Leader Let us pray. Lord Jesus, your suffering and death seem so unfair. It always seems unfair when good people get hurt or lose their jobs or get sick. Please bless those who feel that life is unfair and help them to know that you understand.

All   **Hear our prayer, Lord Jesus. Amen.**

Second Station: Jesus takes up his cross. ❀

Leader Let us pray. Lord Jesus, we pray for those whose crosses are too heavy to carry: for those who are very sick, for those who miss someone who has died, for those who are afraid or sad or lonely. Comfort them and help them carry their crosses.

All   **Hear our prayer, Lord Jesus. Amen.**

Third Station: Jesus falls the first time. ❀

Leader Let us pray. Lord Jesus, falling can be so scary. One minute you're up and the next you're down. Sometimes it hurts. Sometimes people laugh at you. Sometimes no one helps you up. Please be with those people who fall today and help them get up.

All **Hear our prayer, Lord Jesus. Amen.**

Fourth Station: Jesus meets his mother. ❀

Leader Let us pray. Lord Jesus, we forget that you needed your mother, too. Thank you for our mothers and for all those who love us. Bless those who don't have mothers and help them to turn to your mother, Mary, when they need comfort.

All **Hear our prayer, Lord Jesus. Amen.**

Fifth Station: Simon helps Jesus carry the cross. ❀

Leader Let us pray. Lord Jesus, thank you for the people like Simon in our lives: all those who have cared for us and helped us when we needed help. Show us how we can be like Simon for someone else and help us remember that you ask us to help each other.

All **Hear our prayer, Lord Jesus. Amen.**

Sixth Station: Veronica wipes the face of Jesus ❀

Leader Let us pray. Lord Jesus, Veronica wiped your poor face, and your image was left on her cloth. By her kindness she showed your face to the world. Help us to show your face to the world, too, and to do what we can for others who are suffering.

All **Hear our prayer, Lord Jesus. Amen.**

Seventh Station: Jesus falls a second time. ❁

Leader Let us pray. Lord Jesus, sometimes we feel like we fall over and over again. We promise to be good, and we fail. We promise to work harder, and we don't. We promise to change, and we keep doing the same things. Help us know that you love us even when we fall, and help us to get up and try again.

All **Hear our prayer, Lord Jesus. Amen.**

Eighth Station: Jesus comforts the women of Jerusalem. ❁

Leader Let us pray. Lord Jesus, even when you were hurt and tired, you stopped to comfort the women who were so sad. It's hard to think of others when we don't feel good or when we're worried or tired. Help us to think of others when we only want to think of ourselves.

All **Hear our prayer, Lord Jesus. Amen.**

Ninth Station: Jesus falls a third time. ❁

Leader Let us pray. Lord Jesus, you must have been so tired. Please bless those who feel like they cannot go any farther, those who are tempted to quit, those who are just too sad or who are hurting too much. Help them to know that you are with them.

All **Hear our prayer, Lord Jesus. Amen.**

Tenth Station: Jesus' clothes are taken away. ❁

Leader Let us pray. Lord Jesus, the soldiers laughed at you and beat you and didn't care that you hurt. It is hard to understand how some people can be so mean. Please make us kind so that we are never mean to others.

All **Hear our prayer, Lord Jesus. Amen.**

The Eleventh Station: Jesus is nailed to the cross. ☼

Leader Let us pray. Lord Jesus, you forgave those who were hurting you. Help us to forgive people who have hurt us so that we can live with hearts free of bitterness and full of love.

All **Hear our prayer, Lord Jesus. Amen.**

Twelfth Station: Jesus dies on the cross. ☼

Leader Let us pray. Lord Jesus, we pray for those who will die today: the very sick, the very old, those who will die of hunger, those who will die in war. Be with them, and when they die, please bring them to heaven with you.

All **Hear our prayer, Lord Jesus. Amen.**

Thirteenth Station: Jesus is taken down from the cross. ☼

Leader Let us pray. Lord Jesus, your friends were so sad when you died. Please comfort those who are sad because they miss someone who has died, and help them to know that even though they seem gone, those who have died are still with us and love us.

All **Hear our prayer, Lord Jesus. Amen.**

The Fourteenth Station: Jesus is laid in the tomb. ☼

Leader Let us pray. Lord Jesus, the worst thing had happened. You died on a cross, and it was all so unfair, and then they put your body in a tomb. But the best thing happened, too. The tomb was empty on Easter Sunday, because you rose to new life. Help us to remember that sometimes good things can happen, even when everything looks awful.

All **Hear our prayer, Lord Jesus. Amen.**

And we pray together: Glory be to the Father and to the Son and to the Holy Spirit, as it was in the beginning, is now, and ever shall be, world without end. Amen.

First Week of Lent

Then Jesus was led up by the Spirit into the wilderness to be tempted by the devil. He fasted forty days and forty nights, and afterwards he was famished. The tempter came and said to him, "If you are the Son of God, command these stones to become loaves of bread." But he answered, "It is written, 'One does not live by bread alone, but by every word that comes from the mouth of God.'"

Then the devil took him to the holy city and placed him on the pinnacle of the temple, saying to him, "If you are the Son of God, throw yourself down; for it is written, 'He will command his angels concerning you,' and 'On their hands they will bear you up, so that you will not dash your foot against a stone.'" Jesus said to him, "Again it is written, 'Do not put the Lord your God to the test.'"

Again, the devil took him to a very high mountain and showed him all the kingdoms of the world and their splendor; and he said to him, "All these I will give you, if you will fall down and worship me." Jesus said to him, "Away with you, Satan! for it is written, 'Worship the Lord your God, and serve only him.'" Then the devil left him, and suddenly angels came and waited on him.

Worship the Lord your God.

Sunday: First Week of Lent

To think about...

Jesus begins his ministry by first going on a kind of retreat away from the distractions of the world. For the modern family, going away on retreat is not an easy option, but you can make a retreat place in your home. I spent a month in India, and in every Indian home I visited, there was a prayer place. I visited the wealthy and the very poor; Christians, Hindus, Buddhists, and Muslims; and all had their home shrines. In those homes where the spouses were of different religions, there were often two shrines. In one home I visited, there was a shrine where Jesus and Krishna shared an altar. The home shrine was the first place my hosts would show me, always offering me the option of saying a prayer with them. It was lovely.

To do and to talk about...

Create a place of retreat in your home. It doesn't have to be fancy or elaborate. A candle on the dining room table, a picture of the Holy Family or a crucifix in a little niche somewhere—just a place that encourages you to enter into quiet mode. Keep this little booklet there along with your Bible and perhaps a Life of Jesus written for children. Gather the family, and ask God to bless this new quiet place.

Let us pray...

Lord Jesus,
send your Spirit to bless this quiet place.
May it be the center of our home
and a place to go when the world seems harsh.
We pray, Lord, let us be like you.
Amen.

Monday: First Week of Lent

To think about...

Jesus was baptized by his cousin, John, and the Spirit of God descended on Jesus in the form of a dove. After his baptism and before Jesus began his public ministry, this same Holy Spirit led Jesus to a place where he would be tempted by the devil. Why? We'll think about each of the temptations later, but for now, why did Jesus need to be tempted at all? Perhaps it was so that he could fully understand what it is to be human—to be tempted, how hard it is to resist temptation, and how hard it is sometimes to be good. The letter to the Hebrews says, "We do not have a high priest who is unable to sympathize with our weaknesses...." (Hebrews 4:15). Isn't this a comfort? To realize that our Savior so fully understands what it is to be human?

To do and to talk about...

Jesus doesn't ask us to do anything he didn't do. Nor should we ask of others what we do not do ourselves. It's tempting to expect our leaders to work harder than we do, our pastors and teachers to be more virtuous, our children to be more disciplined, our spouses to be more loving, our friends to be more loyal. Talk with your family about those "Do as I say, not as I do" moments, and promise to do what you expect of others. At the very least, it will make you more forgiving.

Let us pray...

Lord Jesus,
help us to live by your golden rule
and do for others what
we want them to do for us.
We pray, Lord, let us be like you.
Amen.

Tuesday: First Week of Lent

To think about...

One of my teenaged sons, upon hearing that Jesus was offered the power to turn stones into bread, mumbled under his breath that Jesus should have taken the deal. I was shocked—not so much at what he said, but that he was listening at all. Before he could lapse back into his usual teenage taciturnity, I whispered, "What do you mean?" He said, in that voice reserved for parents and idiots, "There are a lot of hungry people in the world, Mom." Point well taken. What would be so wrong with taking the deal? If you could turn stones into bread, you would be able to feed the whole world! No more hungry little children with sad eyes and empty bellies. But it doesn't seem to be God's way to do things big. We are encouraged to feed the person on our path, not the whole world. Who is on our path? Maybe a neighbor or someone who comes to our parish food pantry. Maybe a child we meet through an appeal in the mail or at church.

To do and to talk about...

Talk about helping just one person. One possibility is a child sponsorship program where, for a small amount of money each month, you can help feed and educate a child—perhaps a child the same age as one in your family. Do some online research, or if you don't have time today, write down your intention and put it in your alms vessel.

Let us pray...

Lord Jesus,
you rely on us to be your hands and your feet
and your heart in this world.
Help us to help others.
We pray, Lord, let us be like you.
Amen.

Wednesday: First Week of Lent

To think about...

The second temptation is kind of strange. The devil takes Jesus to the highest roof of the temple in Jerusalem and invites him to throw himself down, because God would take care of him. What is this about? The devil is suggesting that Jesus rewrite the rules—both the religious rules about testing God and the rules of nature. Jesus is being offered power over death. "You don't have to suffer," Satan is telling Jesus. "You don't have to die." Who wouldn't be tempted to take this deal? I confess, I would. I don't want to suffer and die. I don't want to watch my loved ones suffer and die. But death, and sometimes suffering, is the way it works; it's part of the plan. We do what we can to avoid it, but in the end, we accept God's invitation to make our suffering into prayer and, eventually, to come home to God.

To do and to talk about...

Children begin thinking about death when they are four or five. You may want to collect a few books that deal with death. There are several I have read to the children in my life: *Up in Heaven,* by Emma Chichester Clark, about the death of a puppy; *The Dead Bird,* by Margaret Wise Brown, about a bird funeral; and *I Wonder What You Do on Your First Day in Heaven,* by Phoebe Welsh, a sensitive and beautifully illustrated book about the death of a child.

Let us pray...

Lord Jesus,
thank you for dying for us.
Please bless our loved ones who have died,
keep them safe with you,
and tell them "Hi" for us.
We pray, Lord, let us be like you.
Amen.

Thursday: First Week of Lent

To think about...

The devil's third temptation is to offer Jesus political power over all the kingdoms of the world. This is the kind of power we long for when we say, "If I were the president...." "If I were the pope...." "If I were the pastor, the principal, the boss...." Or maybe, "If I win the lottery...." Think of how much good you could do! Jesus' response to each temptation is the same: God is my only God. He does things God's way. And God's will for us is to do what it is in our power to do with our resources and talents and not to long for the power, resources, or talents of someone else.

To do and to talk about...

Revisit the idea of sponsoring just one child for whom you could make so much difference. We have been sponsoring four children for several years now. We receive regular letters from them and we write them, too, and we let our grandchildren decorate the letters with their crayons. It means a lot to our little ones to know that the adults in their lives are responding to the need they know exists and also that they have a "special friend" in a faraway place. Today you could talk about whether you want to sponsor a boy or a girl, what age, and in what part of the world. Our six-year-old grandchild can point out Guatemala and India on a globe because that's where her "special friends" live.

Let us pray...

Lord Jesus,
you give us everything we need to do your work in this
world. Help us to recognize the task you set before us,
the person you place on our path.
We pray, Lord, let us be like you.
Amen.

Friday: First Week of Lent

To think about...

Have you been tempted yet to break one of your Lenten promises? How should we deal with that little voice inside that says, "Oh, come on, you can eat a hotdog if you want. God doesn't care if it's Friday"? Or, "Oh, come on, God isn't only inside a church; you don't have to go to Sunday Mass." The best way to deal with that tempter's voice is not to listen to it at all. Put your hands over your ears and go, "la-la-la!" If you engage the voice, you're likely to give in. At the least you will have wasted your time and energy. The other thing you can do is laugh. Tempters hate to be laughed at. Laugh and say, "No thanks, I'm not buying!" And then, put your hands over your ears and say, "la-la-la!"

To do and to talk about...

It's Friday, so no meat today. One of my sons absolutely loathes fish, and it's a real temptation for him to sneak a hotdog or hamburger on Fridays in Lent. Poor kid, especially because the rest of the family doesn't find our parish fish fries penitential. The idea of not eating meat today is partly to eat like the poor—not lobster or expensive fish, but simply and cheaply. Consider making a simple meal and putting the money you save in your alms vessel. If you're thinking of sponsoring a child, find out what the poor eat in that country and try to eat the same thing on Fridays in Lent.

Let us pray...

Lord Jesus,
you ate with your disciples and with sinners, too.
Be with us at our table today
and with those who don't have enough to eat.
We pray, Lord, let us be like you.
Amen.

Prayer

Our Father

It was a surprise to me that this week's Gospel passage doesn't mention anything about prayer. I was sure it said that Jesus prayed for forty days, but it doesn't. One theory—the one I hold—is that prayer is so much a part of the life of the Jewish people that it is presumed. And perhaps this is why Jesus speaks about prayer so little. Only once does he tell the disciples how to pray, and then he gives them the prayer we know as the Lord's Prayer or the Our Father. In just fifty-six words, this prayer helps us pray: (1) to desire God's will; (2) for our needs today; (3) for forgiveness and the ability to forgive others; and (4) for the grace to avoid evil.

I once made a three-day retreat just on the text of the Our Father. You might try saying it one line at a time, and instead of rushing through the whole prayer all at once, linger on each phrase and think about what it means. Teach your children the Our Father and say it with them every day, perhaps as part of their bedtime prayers.

Our Father, who art in heaven,
hallowed be thy name;
thy kingdom come,
thy will be done on earth
as it is in heaven.
Give us this day our daily bread
and forgive us our trespasses,
as we forgive those who trespass against us
and lead us not into temptation,
but deliver us from evil.
Amen.

Fun Page

Cryptogram: Words to Live By

Solve the code and live by it.

A	B	C	D	E	F	G	H	I	J	K	L	M	N	O	P	Q	R	S	T	U	V	W	X	Y	Z
15	17	24	5	20	19	4	9	6	21	2	22	18	13	11	23	7	3	14	10	1	25	16	8	26	12

11 13 20   5 11 20 14   13 11 10   22 6 25 20

17 26   17 3 20 15 5   15 22 11 13 20 ,

17 1 10   17 26   20 25 20 3 26   16 11 3 5

10 9 15 10   24 11 18 20 14   19 3 11 18   10 9 20

18 11 1 10 9   11 19   4 11 5 .

Solution on page 2

Second Week of Lent

Six days later, Jesus took with him Peter and James and his brother John and led them up a high mountain, by themselves. And he was transfigured before them, and his face shone like the sun, and his clothes became dazzling white. Suddenly there appeared to them Moses and Elijah, talking with him. Then Peter said to Jesus, "Lord, it is good for us to be here; if you wish, I will make three dwellings here, one for you, one for Moses, and one for Elijah." While he was still speaking, suddenly a bright cloud overshadowed them, and from the cloud a voice said, "This is my Son, the Beloved; with him I am well pleased; listen to him!" When the disciples heard this, they fell to the ground and were overcome by fear. But Jesus came and touched them, saying, "Get up and do not be afraid." And when they looked up, they saw no one except Jesus himself alone.

As they were coming down the mountain, Jesus ordered them, "Tell no one about the vision until after the Son of Man has been raised from the dead."

"This is my Son, the Beloved... listen to him!"

Sunday: Second Week of Lent

To think about...

I've witnessed transfigurations. I direct a choir, and sometimes their faces change when they sing. These ordinary, rather lumpy people begin to glow, their eyes full of light, their faces bright with the joy of harmony. And once I watched a farmer and his wife bring up the gifts at Mass—both with rough, calloused hands—carrying the bread and wine like something precious, moving with the grace of dancers. I've watched as people receive Holy Communion, and sometimes they become brighter, softer, vulnerable. And the faces of those who come forward to venerate the cross on Good Friday—those faces could break your heart. Transfiguration is what happens when a baby is brought into the room, or enemies shake hands, or two people fall in love. The hardness, the weariness, the wariness is gone, and for an instant, our faces glow, and we are as we are meant to be.

To do and to talk about...

Go to Mass today and remember falling in love. Remember holding your child for the first time. Children love to be told "their story." Get out the wedding pictures and the baby pictures and show your children how much everyone changes. Tell them about the first time you held them and how you felt.

Let us pray...

Lord Jesus,
help me to see your face in each person I meet this week,
your work in each task set before me,
your will in every sudden change of plans.
We pray, Lord, let us be like you.
Amen.

Monday: Second Week of Lent

To think about...

Who really changed? Jesus the Christ, the Messiah, the Lord of Lords and King of Kings, the One who was at the beginning of time and who will be at the end? Or was the change in Peter, John, and James? I can imagine Jesus walking along the dusty roads of Palestine, shining like the sun, maybe conversing with a long-dead prophet or two. But folks didn't notice. They only saw the carpenter's son. We see what we want to see, what we expect to see. I figure what could have happened up on that mountain is that the eyes of the disciples were opened to the way Jesus was all the time. They were given a glimpse of the true truth, a deeper reality. For just a moment they were given "resurrection eyes."

To do and to talk about...

Practice seeing with your resurrection eyes. Today ask Jesus to help you see others (and yourself) as he sees us—as brothers and sisters of Jesus and each other. Today let's try to see without any dark filters of resentment or negative expectation or the fuzziness of distraction. Then we might see each other as we really are—shining like the sun and full of light.

Let us pray...

Lord Jesus,
open our eyes to see your face;
open our ears to hear your voice;
open our hearts to receive each other
as a gift from you.
Help us to see as you see.
We pray, Lord, let us be like you.
Amen.

THE FAMILY RESOURCES CENTER

Family Resources Center
415 NE Monroe,
Peoria, IL 61603 (309) 839-2287

Tuesday: Second Week of Lent

To think about...

Peter, James, and John caught a glimpse of Jesus as he really was. Seeing each other as we really are is difficult if we're too distracted. What are we looking at instead of each other? Ray Bradbury wrote *Fahrenheit 451* back in the sixties. The setting is far in the future when people wouldn't read anymore—in fact, weren't allowed to read—and television screens took up the entire wall of a room. The goal of every family was to have screens on all four walls of their "parlor," and they referred to the actors as their "parlor families." Maybe Bradbury's future has arrived. Children now watch child actors on huge plasma TVs more than they play with the children in their neighborhood. And parents rush their children to bed without reading them a book or singing to them or saying night prayers just so they don't miss an eight o'clock show.

To do and to talk about...

If your television is on all the time, try weaning yourself off it for periods of time. Start with meals. Maybe work up to a TV-free evening and eventually, a TV-free weekend. Plan something else instead—baking cookies, doing some of the activities in this book. You can always watch a rerun of your favorite show. There are no reruns with your children. It's now or never.

Let us pray...

Lord Jesus,
give us the courage to put away distractions,
even to risk being bored,
so that we might begin to enjoy
the company of those we love.
We pray, Lord, let us be like you.
Amen.

Wednesday: Second Week of Lent

To think about...

I remember a glorious summer evening with my young sons in the park. The three of them were happily running along the crest of a hill. I saw them silhouetted against the brilliant sunset and suddenly knew that they would someday be running into their own future, no longer little boys, but men. It brought tears to my eyes—tears of grief and joy and wonder and...fear. We know that someday this life will be no more. Our faith tells us that the end is not the end, but a new beginning. The tragedy is when we don't pay attention, when we are too distracted to notice and remember the gift of today.

To do and to talk about...

If you find that life is passing you by too quickly and you can't remember what you did just last week, consider keeping a "house journal." I started this practice several years ago. Every night I note the weather, how many eggs we collected from our chickens, how much money we spent and on what, and then the highlights of the day. I keep this journal on my laptop, so I insert digital photos. Each month I print it out and place the pages in a three-ring binder which I present to my husband at Christmas. We love having this record of the improvements to our home and the growth of our garden and our grandchildren. I do regret that I didn't start this practice when my boys were young.

Let us pray...

Lord Jesus,
help us to notice and appreciate all that
is precious so that when our final hour is upon us
we will remember that all that is good lasts forever.
We pray, Lord, let us be like you.
Amen.

Thursday: Second Week of Lent

To think about...

Did you ever wonder why Jesus chose who he did to be his apostles? Peter, for instance. No disrespect intended, but he seems so ill-suited to the job. In response to the transfiguration of Jesus, Peter babbles on about building three little houses, one each for Jesus, Moses, and Elijah. Luke's Gospel even goes so far as to say that Peter didn't know what he was talking about. I wonder if Peter didn't want to somehow put this experience in terms he could understand. After all, there's his friend Jesus, lit up like a Christmas tree and chatting with two long-dead heroes of the Bible. That had to be pretty awesome, but confusing, too. Sometimes when we can't stretch enough, we try instead to keep God as small as we are. We decide what God can forgive and what is unforgiveable, who God can save and who is beyond salvation, what is possible and what is not.

To do and to talk about...

Challenge your children to a "dream contest." After they lay out their wishes for the latest electronic gizmo, dare them to dream even bigger. How would they make their world a better place if they could? If they were God?

Let us pray...

Lord Jesus,
we know our good dreams come from you,
and we dare to dream of
a family, a neighborhood, a church, a world,
that are safe, peaceful, holy, happy places for everyone.
We pray, Lord, let us be like you.
Amen

Friday: Second Week of Lent

To think about...

After Peter goes on about building three little houses, what happens? A voice from the clouds says, "Peter, hush. You're missing it. This is my Son. Listen to him!" (Well, those weren't the voice's exact words, but that was the drift.) I experienced an unusually peaceful Lent the year I lost my voice. (Okay, I can already hear my sons when they read this: "Hey it was pretty peaceful for us, too, Mom.") Anyway, I lost my voice. Totally. I could only whisper. My granddaughter was five then, and she responded to me in whispers. So did some adults, even on the phone. It was pretty funny, but it was a gentling experience. I found myself noticing more, listening more. Even Jesus needed to go off by himself once in a while where it was quiet, and this was before cell phones, the Internet, MP3 players, and TV.

To do and to talk about...

Have you given anymore thought to turning off the TV? I know when you're used to it, the silence can be deafening. Try it though, at least during meals. If anyone complains—and they probably will—try this math exercise with them. Multiply the number of hours of TV per day by three hundred sixty-five. Then divide by twenty-four. This equals the full days per year of watching TV. The average American family watches TV two solid months out of every year. If you live to seventy-five, that's a whopping twelve solid years of watching other people's lives. (Remember—no meat today.)

Let us pray...

Lord Jesus,
quiet our minds and our hearts, help us to not be afraid
of silent times because then we might hear your voice
whispering inside of us. We pray, Lord, let us be like you.
Amen.

Prayer

Glory Be

Henri Nouwen once said that people are killing each other all the time. He explained, "No one is shot with a gun who isn't first shot with a word. And no one is shot with a word who isn't first shot with a thought."

I hope I would never purposely kill anyone, but I confess I do have unkind thoughts. If not unkind thoughts, there is too often a whining undercurrent going on: "Why does it have to rain today?" "Why is he always late?" "I'm hungry." "I'm tired." "I want." "I need." And if not whining, there is certainly a lot of unnecessary chatter—not unlike in Sunday's Gospel passage when Peter has to be hushed up by the voice in the cloud and told to listen. How can we quiet our minds enough to listen for God's voice?

Glory Be is a simple prayer of praise, or "word of glory," that can serve as a kind of mantra or focusing phrase. Repeating it reminds us that the world is bigger than our immediate concerns, that God is in charge, that what we do and say and think should contribute to the glory in the world, not the dismal gloominess that we can find ourselves mired in. Teach this prayer to your children and try praying it in place of whatever you think or speak that doesn't make the world a better place. A day full of Glory Be's might just be what the world needs.

Glory be to the Father,
and to the Son,
and to the Holy Spirit,
as it was in the beginning,
is now,
and ever shall be,
world without end.
Amen.

Hidden Message: Are You Listening?

Find the message from Sunday's Gospel:

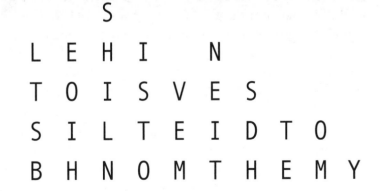

Make a phrase from the jumbled letters under the grid. The letters appearing in each column of the completed phrase are scrambled directly under that column.

Solution on page 2

Third Week of Lent

Note: For the next three Sundays, you may hear a different Gospel at Mass. The Gospel passages in this book are part of "Cycle A" of the liturgical calendar which is read at least every three years, but a Catholic parish may read Gospels from "Cycle A" every year because they emphasize so well the themes of baptism and new life—that new life we celebrate at Easter.

Jesus came to a Samaritan city called Sychar, near the plot of ground that Jacob had given to his son Joseph. Jacob's well was there, and Jesus, tired out by his journey, was sitting by the well. It was about noon.

A Samaritan woman came to draw water, and Jesus said to her, "Give me a drink." (His disciples had gone to the city to buy food.) The Samaritan woman said to him, "How is it that you, a Jew, ask a drink of me, a woman of Samaria?" (Jews do not share things in common with Samaritans.) Jesus answered her, "If you knew the gift of God, and who it is that is saying to you, 'Give me a drink,' you would have asked him, and he would have given you living water." The woman said to him, "Sir, you have no bucket, and the well is deep. Where do you get that living water? Are you greater than our ancestor Jacob, who gave us the well, and with his sons and his flocks drank from it?" Jesus said to her, "Everyone who drinks of this water will be thirsty again, but those who drink of the water that I will give them will never be thirsty. The water that I will give will become in them a spring of water gushing up to eternal life." The woman said to him, "Sir, give me this water, so that I may never be thirsty or have to keep coming here to draw water."

Jesus said to her, "Go, call your husband, and come back." The woman answered him, "I have no husband." Jesus said to her, "You are right in saying, 'I have no husband'; for you have had five husbands, and the one you have now is not your husband. What you have said is true!" The woman said, "I see that you are a prophet. Our ancestors worshiped on this mountain, but you say that the place where people must worship is in Jerusalem." Jesus said to her, "Woman, believe me, the hour

is coming when you will worship the Father neither on this mountain nor in Jerusalem. God is spirit, and those who worship him must worship in spirit and truth." The woman said to him, "I know that Messiah is coming" (who is called Christ). "When he comes, he will proclaim all things to us." Jesus said to her, "I am he, the one who is speaking to you."

Just then his disciples came. They were astonished that he was speaking with a woman, but no one said, "What do you want?" or, "Why are you speaking with her?" Then the woman left her water jar and went back to the city. She said to the people, "Come and see a man who told me everything I have ever done! He cannot be the Messiah, can he?"

Many Samaritans from that city believed in him because of the woman's testimony, "He told me everything I have ever done." So when the Samaritans came to him, they asked him to stay with them; and he stayed there two days. And many more believed because of his word. They said to the woman, "It is no longer because of what you said that we believe, for we have heard for ourselves, and we know that this is truly the Savior of the world."

Sunday: Third Week of Lent

To think about...

Water. We take it for granted. Turn on the tap and there it is. We need never be thirsty. We think of women gathering at the village well as an ancient practice, but consider these statistics issued by the United Nations: more than five hundred million people live without access to clean water. In these places, people—almost always women and children—walk an average of three-and-a-half miles every day to get water, often from a well like the woman in today's Gospel. It's not just in ancient times that people carried their water long distances. As you read this, women and children in many parts of the world are gathering at wells and preparing for a long walk home.

To do and to talk about...

Except for the daily requirement of milk for the little ones— okay, and a little coffee or tea for the caffeine-dependent— drink water. Put a (non-breakable) container near every water tap in the house—including the bathtub and the toilet—and every time you turn on the water or flush, put a penny in that container. (Alternately, put a piece of paper and a pencil at each tap and make one mark for every time you use water. Count up the marks at the end of the week and collect a penny for each mark.) Put the money you collect in your alms vessel for the poor.

Let us pray...

Lord Jesus,
we give you thanks for the gift of pure, clean water
and for those who work to keep our water safe.
Help us to extend this simple blessing
to those who suffer for lack of clean water.
We pray, Lord, let us be like you.
Amen.

Monday: Third Week of Lent

To think about...

In the small town where our parish church is located, the folks were put on a sudden "boil order" because E. coli was found in the water. Soon the stores were sold out of bottled water. We live in the country with our own well, so we responded with a "water party." Friends brought their jugs and bottles to fill and a dish to share, and we had a great time. The boil order lasted less than a week, but it made people think about what it would be like to live where there was no readily available pure water. So many people in our world suffer and die from illnesses caused by impure water and lack of sanitation. Doesn't it seem strange that we have the technology to do so many amazing things and yet cannot find a way to provide clean water to all the children of the world?

To do and to talk about...

To find out what other people are doing to provide clean water everywhere, check out www.worldwaterday.org. You might consider participating in one of their many efforts sometime between March 22 (International World Water Day) and April 22 (Earth Day). Don't forget to collect your pennies for every time you turn on the tap or flush.

Let us pray...

Lord Jesus,
thank you for all the kind and energetic people
who work to help others.
We want to be one of those people.
Fill us with your love and your grace so that
we can reach out to others in your name.
We pray, Lord, let us be like you.
Amen.

Tuesday: Third Week of Lent

To think about...

Jesus often described himself as food and drink: "bread of life," "living water." It is through Jesus that every hunger, every desire, is satisfied. What do you hunger for? What do you really want? I'm reminded of an incident in my middle son's life. A classmate had three extra tickets to a local amusement park. He invited three other boys from the class, and my son was all upset that he wasn't invited. Funny thing was this quiet son of mine absolutely hated amusement parks and wouldn't go on a ride if you paid him. If we can teach our young people to notice what they really want, they might not get so sidetracked by what they think should be fun or desirable. People who do not know their deepest desires are like the runner who, when asked, "Where are you going?" answers, "I don't know, but I'm getting there faster than you are."

To do and to talk about...

Schedule a talk with your family about deepest desires. If you know you've got a long drive coming up, the car is a good place to get introspective. If you're at home, maybe it will help to let everyone write or draw as they think about what they really want. Ask Jesus to show you what's deep in your heart and to guide your desires. (Don't forget those pennies!)

Let us pray...

Lord Jesus,
our good dreams, our deepest desires, come from you.
Help us to know what we really want, what you made us
to do and be in this world, and then help us to find the
way to becoming the best person we can be.
We pray, Lord, let us be like you.
Amen.

Wednesday: Third Week of Lent

To think about...

What do we know about the woman at the well? She was married a few times—we don't know why. It was the custom for women to go to the well together early in the morning before it got hot, but she's there by herself at noon, so maybe the other women avoided her. She was probably pretty brave, not only because of the way she spoke with Jesus so honestly, but because of something else remarkable. After she talked with Jesus, she ran to the townspeople and said, "Come and see a man who told me everything I have ever done!" Can you imagine saying something like that to people who didn't treat you very well? If I met someone who told me everything I ever did, I might not want everyone to know about it. Maybe the woman was just relieved and so happy that she couldn't keep it to herself. That's what we feel when our secrets are finally known—relieved and happy.

To do and to talk about...

Lent is a time when we should celebrate the sacrament of penance and reconciliation—go to confession. Start making a plan to go together as a family, either at your parish's regularly scheduled confession times or, if possible, to a communal penance service in your area. Today just research the dates and times and get it on the family calendar. (And keep collecting those pennies.)

Let us pray...

Lord Jesus,
we know we can tell you anything
and that you will still love us.
Help us look into our hearts and remember all of our words
and actions that are not something you would say or do.
We pray, Lord, let us be like you.
Amen.

Thursday: Third Week of Lent

To think about...

Why do good people do bad things? Even Saint Paul wrote about this problem in his letter to the Christians in Rome: "I do not understand my own actions. For I do not do what I want, but I do the very thing I hate" (Romans 7:15). Sin is real. But you know what? Forgiveness is real, too. As Catholics, we have the sacrament of penance and reconciliation, commonly known as confession. Many Catholics celebrate this sacrament regularly and can't imagine being without it. Others are hesitant—some out of fear, some out of shame. Let me tell you, as a veteran penitent, there's no reason to be afraid. If your pastor is not someone with a good "bedside manner," go to a different priest. As for shame...fugeddaboutit. Seriously, it's unlikely that you could tell a priest something he hasn't heard before, and we are all sinners. All! Remember the prayer we say before we receive Holy Communion? "Lord, I am not worthy to receive you, but only say the word and I shall be healed." None of us is worthy, but all of us are loved.

To do and to talk about...

Have you put confession on your family calendar yet? Please do. If you can find a communal penance service, these are great experiences for children. There they discover that everyone needs to seek forgiveness—their friends, teachers, coaches, everyone. Plan on a little celebration afterwards like going out for ice cream or pizza.

Let us pray...

Lord Jesus,
give us such a strong desire to be good
that we will admit our failings and do all that we can
to grow into the person you call us to be.
We pray, Lord, let us be like you.
Amen.

Friday: Third Week of Lent

To think about...

When we do something bad the first time, we feel bad about it. But the next time, it's a little easier, and after that, doing something bad gets easier and easier. Feeling bad about doing bad things is a good thing. If we didn't, it would mean that our conscience is pretty sluggish and our soul would be really in danger. One way to keep your conscience in good shape is the "examination of conscience." Every night before you go to bed, ask God to help you remember your day. Then if you remember doing, saying, or thinking something you shouldn't have, tell God you're sorry and ask for help to do better the next day. I can't think of a better practice for busy folks who want to be good parents and for children who are being raised to be good Christians.

To do and to talk about...

I'll bet you're tired of making a mark or finding a penny every time you use water, aren't you? If you did this every day this week, good for you! You can stop now. Collect all the pennies and put them in your alms vessel and maybe try to find some way to participate in the effort to provide clean water to all the world's children. From now on, when you drink water, say a short prayer for those who are without clean, pure water. (No meat today.)

Let us pray...

Lord Jesus,
we have come to the end of the work week,
more aware of those who live without what
we take for granted.
Thank you for our blessings.
Give us now the desire to share with others.
We pray, Lord, let us be like you.
Amen.

Prayer

Act of Contrition

The woman at the well knew she was a sinner. Only when she met Jesus did she realize that, however great her sin, God's love is greater. We meet Jesus in the sacrament of penance, and there we confess our sins and meet the loving grace of God. The Act of Contrition is part of the sacrament of penance, and it's a good prayer to memorize. Here are two versions of this prayer. Learn one of them by heart and keep it there—in your heart.

Traditional Act of Contrition

O my God,
I am heartily sorry
*   for having offended thee,*
and I detest all my sins,
because I dread the loss
*   of heaven and*
*   the pains of hell,*
but most of all because
*   they offend thee, my God,*
who are all good and
*   deserving of all my love.*
I firmly resolve,
with the help of thy grace,
to confess my sins,
to do penance,
and to amend my life.
Amen.

Act of Contrition for Children

My God,
I am sorry for my sins
*   with all my heart.*
In choosing to do wrong
*   and failing to do good,*
I have sinned against you
whom I should love
*   above all things.*
I promise to try, with your help,
to do penance,
to sin no more,
and to avoid whatever
*   leads me to sin.*
Amen.

Fun Page

Crossword: Thirsty for God

Find Key Words from
Sunday's Gospel.

ACROSS
1. well named after him
4. witness
5. Holy City
7. followers
9. adore
12. to be saved
13. take a trip
14. forebears
16. best for thirst

DOWN
2. for carrying water
3. source of water
4. need a drink
6. God's anointed
8. Jacob's son
10. spokesperson
11. Jesus
15. Northern Palestine

Solution on page 2

Fourth Week of Lent

As [Jesus] walked along, he saw a man blind from birth. His disciples asked him, "Rabbi, who sinned, this man or his parents, that he was born blind?" Jesus answered, "Neither this man nor his parents sinned; he was born blind so that God's works might be revealed in him. We must work the works of him who sent me while it is day; night is coming when no one can work. As long as I am in the world, I am the light of the world." When he had said this, he spat on the ground and made mud with the saliva and spread the mud on the man's eyes, saying to him, "Go, wash in the pool of Siloam" (which means Sent). Then he went and washed and came back able to see. The neighbors and those who had seen him before as a beggar began to ask, "Is this not the man who used to sit and beg?" Some were saying, "It is he." Others were saying, "No, but it is someone like him." He kept saying, "I am the man."

They brought to the Pharisees the man who had formerly been blind. Now it was a sabbath day when Jesus made the mud and opened his eyes. Then the Pharisees also began to ask him how he had received his sight. He said to them, "He put mud on my eyes. Then I washed, and now I see." Some of the Pharisees said, "This man is not from God, for he does not observe the sabbath." But oth-

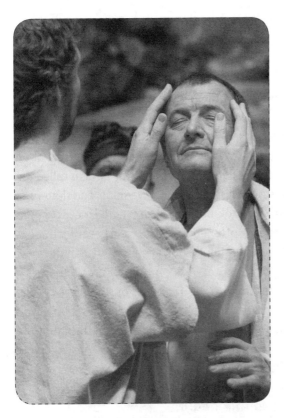

anyone opened the eyes of a person born blind. If this man were not from God, he could do nothing." They answered him, "You were born entirely in sins, and are you trying to teach us?" And they drove him out.

Jesus heard that they had driven him out, and when he found him, he said, "Do you believe in the Son of Man?" He answered, "And who is he, sir? Tell me, so that I may believe in him." Jesus said to him, "You have seen him, and the one speaking with you is he." He said, "Lord, I believe." And he worshiped him. Jesus said, "I came into this world for judgment so that those who do not see may see, and those who do see may become blind." Some of the Pharisees near him heard this and said to him, "Surely we are not blind, are we?" Jesus said to them, "If you were blind, you would not have sin. But now that you say, 'We see,' your sin remains."

ers said, "How can a man who is a sinner perform such signs?" And they were divided. So they said again to the blind man, "What do you say about him? It was your eyes he opened." He said, "He is a prophet."

"You do not know where he comes from, and yet he opened my eyes. We know that God does not listen to sinners, but he does listen to one who worships him and obeys his will. Never since the world began has it been heard that

Sunday: Fourth Week of Lent

To think about...

In the ancient world, there were only two sources of light: the sun and fire. Without either of them, the world was a dark, dark place. I don't think we can experience darkness like that—except for maybe in a closet. Now, even in the middle of a desert or an ocean, we still see the reflected lights of cities far away. Jesus is called the light of the world. The Jesus light is illuminating, warming, and flattering, too. In the light of Jesus, we look our best, like we do by candlelight. The less-becoming parts are softened somehow, and everyone looks beautiful. Maybe that's how we should look at each other—in the most pleasing light possible. At the Easter Vigil on Holy Saturday, there is a fire, and from it the Easter candle is lit. From this one gigantic candle, all the people in the congregation light their little candles. I hope you plan to go this year and take your children. The passing of the light from that single candle to all the people and the sight of all those glowing faces is an unforgettable experience.

To do and to talk about...

When our children were young, we always ate by candlelight, and we still do. It's calming, and we find that we want to linger at the table. Eat by candlelight tonight. (Continue to turn off the harsh light of the TV while you eat.)

Let us pray...

Lord Jesus,
you are the light of the world
and the light of our lives.
Reveal to us what we need to see
so that we may always live in your light.
We pray, Lord, let us be like you.
Amen.

Monday: Fourth Week of Lent

To think about...

In Sunday's Gospel, Jesus and his disciples come upon a blind man. The disciples want to know whose sin is responsible—the man himself or his parents. Aren't we like that sometimes? Aren't we tempted to blame the victim or the victim's parents? Whatever the illness or condition—cancer, heart disease, injury—we want to know if they smoked, drank too much, worked too much, ate a lot of bacon, were wearing their seat belt. Sometimes we are responsible for our pain and suffering. There are measures we can and should take to care for ourselves and our loved ones. But sometimes bad things just happen. Probably the best approach is to give others the benefit of the doubt along with our compassion and concern. At the same time, maybe we should look carefully at our own condition and, instead of playing the victim, ask what we can do to prevent or heal illness or infirmity.

To do and to talk about...

Are there situations when you are tempted to unfairly blame the victim? Why do we do this? What should we do instead? Is there anything about yourself that you wish you could change? If so, can you give that desire to Jesus and ask for help in creating a better, healthier, happier you?

Let us pray...

Lord Jesus,
you healed the man born blind.
Open our eyes to what we can do
to care for others
and to care for ourselves.
We pray, Lord, let us be like you.
Amen.

Tuesday: Fourth Week of Lent

To think about...

Jesus said that the man's blindness was "so that God's works could be revealed in him." Fortunately, this blind man was not so involved in his own suffering that he couldn't gratefully accept healing. And when he was healed, he didn't spend time mourning the years without his sight, but instead, rejoiced in the glory of light—first and foremost, the light of Jesus' own face shining on him. That's what we can always control—not what happens to us, but what we make of it, what we do with it. This was the insight of Viktor Frankl, Jewish psychiatrist from Vienna, holocaust survivor, and author of *Man's Search for Meaning.* He endured the worst deprivation and cruelty, and what helped him survive was realizing that "The last of human freedoms" (the one no one can take away) "is the ability to choose one's attitude in a given set of circumstances."

To do and to talk about...

Some kind children learn how it feels to be teased and won't tease others. Some good parents learn from bad parenting. Some employees are laid off and discover that the new task waiting for them is what they were meant to do all along. What has been hard or sad or cruel in your life that you have turned into an opportunity for growth? Do you know what it's called when you grow and become more alive after experiencing something difficult? It's life from death—resurrection!

Let us pray...

Lord Jesus,
heal our blindness and open our eyes to your presence
in hard times and in good so that we may grow into that
unique person we were born to be.
We pray, Lord, let us be like you.
Amen.

Wednesday: Fourth Week of Lent

To think about...

I made a collage inspired by a quote from William Morris: "Have nothing in your homes that you do not know to be useful or believe to be beautiful." I took pictures of ordinary household objects, but from different angles than we usually see them. There is a close-up of a glass doorknob, the back of a rocker made of lovely wood, the wicker top of a hamper, one patch on a quilt. It turned out pretty nice and hangs in our living room. A favorite game of my grandchildren is to ask guests to find those objects in the house. Children are better than adults at this game. They see with their fresh eyes what we don't expect to see with our mature eyes. When Jesus tells us to be like little children, I think this is kind of what he means—to walk through the world with eyes wide open to the beauty that is all around us, to expect goodness everywhere, to delight in the ordinary.

To do and to talk about...

If you have a camera, you might like to try making a collage of your own of the ordinary, but beautiful, objects in your home. Or try seeing your home from a different angle—from the vantage point of each member of the family. What do you see when you're crawling? Or walking around only three or four feet tall? Or in a wheelchair? World looks different, doesn't it?

Let us pray...

Lord Jesus,
open our eyes to a new way of seeing
so that we recognize the beautiful
in this ordinary world
and the blessings of an ordinary day.
We pray, Lord, let us be like you.
Amen.

Thursday: Fourth Week of Lent

To think about...

A man was riding on the subway in New York City when another man got on with his three children. The kids were just wild—running around the car, jumping on the seats, disturbing the other passengers. The first man was getting more and more irritated and finally approached the father and asked, "Don't you see how your children are behaving? They're bothering everybody. Aren't you going to do something?" The father of the kids looked up confused, obviously just noticing what was going on. He apologized and said, "I'm so sorry. We just came from the funeral home where we're making arrangements. My wife died yesterday. I guess the kids are just confused by it all." Then he called his kids over, and they sat down quietly. The first man felt awful, and all his irritation melted away, to be replaced by concern. "I'm so sorry for your loss," he said. "Is there anything I can do?"

To do and to talk about...

We often find ourselves irritated by the behavior of others. Another driver cuts us off; a cashier keeps talking on the phone while we wait; a customer is rude; a teacher yells for no reason; some kid is always teasing everybody. Identify one instance of another's irritating behavior, and then list five reasons why that person might have behaved that way. The practice of imagining reasons for people's behavior is a good one to instill in your children.

Let us pray...

Lord Jesus,
open the eyes of our imagination and help us to see others
as you see them and then give them
the benefit of the doubt when their behavior hurts us.
We pray, Lord, let us be like you.
Amen.

Friday: Fourth Week of Lent

To think about...

A rabbi asked a question of his disciples, "When does night end and day begin?"

"When it becomes light enough to walk along the path without the use of a lantern," said one.

"When you can see someone approaching in the distance," said another.

"When the stars fade from the sky," said a third. The rabbi shook his head. "When you look into a stranger's face," he said, "and recognize him or her as your dear brother or sister, only then has the day begun."

Every person we meet is placed on our path by God. If we listen closely, perhaps we can hear God introducing us to each other: "Meet my beloved son or daughter. I will be so happy if you love each other."

To do and to talk about...

When we look at each other with our resurrection eyes, we see people as Jesus sees them. Practice seeing this way, particularly people you either don't like so much or those you really don't see—the mail carrier, the other driver, the person behind us in line. How can you put this new kind of seeing in action? Is there someone you've failed to acknowledge or thank? Someone you're avoiding? Someone you won't forgive? Make plans to change that, won't you?

Let us pray...

Lord Jesus,
open my eyes to see
your face in each person I meet today,
your will in each task set before me,
and give me the grace to do as you would do.
We pray, Lord, let us be like you.
Amen.

Prayer

Hail Mary

Jesus healed the man born blind, giving him not only his sight to see the world around him, but also the grace to see Jesus for who he really is.

Of all the human beings who have ever lived, Jesus' mother, Mary, saw him the most clearly—her child, the God-man Jesus. We pray to Mary to help us see clearly, to find Jesus in the faces of each other, to find brothers and sisters even among our enemies, to find God's creative love in the world around us.

We may pray to all the saints and all those gone before us, including our loved ones who have died, asking them to intercede or pray for us. Teach your children that they can ask Mary to pray for them, and help them memorize this prayer that begins with the greeting of the angel.

Hail Mary, full of grace,
the Lord is with you.
Blessed are you among women
and blessed is the fruit of your womb, Jesus.
Holy Mary, Mother of God,
pray for us sinners now
and at the hour of our death.
Amen.

Hidden Objects: Find the Fishes

A fish was an early symbol of Jesus. How good are your eyes? Are your eyes open to find Jesus everywhere? Find and color the hidden fish in the picture below. *(Hint: There are twelve of them, one for each of the first Apostles.)*

Fifth Week of Lent

Martha and Mary sent a message to Jesus, "Lord, he whom you love is ill." But when Jesus heard it, he said, "This illness does not lead to death; rather it is for God's glory, so that the Son of God may be glorified through it." Accordingly, though Jesus loved Martha and her sister and Lazarus, after having heard that Lazarus was ill, he stayed two days longer in the place where he was.

Then after this he said to the disciples, "Let us go to Judea again."

When Jesus arrived, he found that Lazarus had already been in the tomb four days. When Martha heard that Jesus was coming, she went and met him, while Mary stayed at home. Martha said to Jesus, "Lord, if you had been here, my brother would not have died. But even now I know that God will give you whatever you ask of him." Jesus said to her, "Your brother will rise again." Martha said to him, "I know that he will rise again in the resurrection on the last day." Jesus said to her, "I am the resurrection and the life. Those who believe in me, even though they die, will live, and everyone who lives and believes in me will never die. Do you believe this?" She said to him, "Yes, Lord, I believe that you are the Messiah, the Son of God, the one coming into the world."

When Jesus saw her weeping,

a cave, and a stone was lying against it. Jesus said, "Take away the stone." Martha, the sister of the dead man, said to him, "Lord, already there is a stench because he has been dead four days." Jesus said to her, "Did I not tell you that if you believed, you would see the glory of God?" So they took away the stone. And Jesus looked upward and said, "Father, I thank you for having heard me. I knew that you always hear me, but I have said this for the sake of the crowd standing here, so that they may believe that you sent me." When he had said this, he cried with a loud voice, "Lazarus, come out!" The dead man came out, his hands and feet bound with strips of cloth, and his face wrapped in a cloth. Jesus said to them, "Unbind him, and let him go."

Many of the Jews therefore, who had come with Mary and had seen what Jesus did, believed in him.

and the Jews who came with her also weeping, he was greatly disturbed in spirit and deeply moved. He said, "Where have you laid him?" They said to him, "Lord, come and see." Jesus began to weep. So the Jews said, "See how he loved him!" But some of them said, "Could not he who opened the eyes of the blind man have kept this man from dying?"

Then Jesus, again greatly disturbed, came to the tomb. It was

Sunday: Fifth Week of Lent

To think about...

Martha's cry of protest to the Lord is so touching: "Lord, if you had been here, my brother wouldn't have died." In other words, "Where were you when I needed you?" This is the cry of weeping parents for their child in pain, a child who loses a pet or whose family is in trouble, someone whose loved one dies suddenly. "Where were you?!" Later in the story, Jesus is so moved by the grief of Martha and her friends that he is "troubled in spirit" and he, too, weeps. And that's exactly where Jesus is when we are grieving. He is right beside us, sharing our grief. We are blessed that our savior is one who weeps with us.

To do or to talk about...

If you know of someone who has lost a loved one or has had some recent bad news, plan today to send them a card. A note of sympathy when we're hurting can mean a lot. How are you doing with your Lenten promises? We're getting close to the end now—only two weeks to go. Talk today with your family about how you're doing and, if you're slipping a bit, renew your promises.

Let us pray...

Lord Jesus,
when we're sad or troubled,
sometimes we're tempted to think
that you have forgotten about us.
Help us to feel your presence with us
when we most need a friend
and please be with those who need comfort today.
We pray, Lord, let us be like you.
Amen.

Monday: Fifth Week of Lent

To think about...

Do you know this old joke? The doctor said to her patient: "There's good news and bad news. The good news is that you're going to heaven. The bad news is that you're going soon." Doesn't it seem like we should live our life ready for death? It's the one sure thing—well, one of two—death and taxes. (That's an old joke, too.) We should live ready to be welcomed into heaven at any time. Death is scary—even Jesus thought so, as he prayed in the garden. Death is sad—even Jesus thought so, as he said goodbye to his friends. But death is part of this life, and try as we might, we don't call the shots on this one. How do we live to be ready for death? Fully. Joyfully. Kindly. Clinging to what lasts—faith, hope, and love, writes Saint Paul, and the greatest of these is love.

To do or to talk about...

Sometime soon, sit with your family and make a "bucket list." It's a list of things you want to do before you "kick the bucket." But you can also make such a list of things you want to do this summer or while your children are still young. A bucket list is another way of getting in touch with your deepest desires.

Let us pray...

Lord Jesus,
by dying you destroyed the power of death
to separate us from all that we love.
Help us to live fully this precious life
so that when it is our turn to pass from this world,
we can joyfully leap into your arms.
We pray, Lord, let us be like you.
Amen.

Tuesday: Fifth Week of Lent

To think about...

How do we explain heaven to a child? There's a lovely story of a pastor who was asked about heaven by an anxious parishioner. As they were talking, there was a scratching sound at the door. The pastor opened the door only to have his dog bound into the room, wagging his tail and barking his enthusiastic greeting. The pastor turned to the parishioner and said, "You see, my dog did not know what was on the other side of this door except only that his master is here. We don't know what heaven is like, but we know our Master is there, and so we shouldn't be afraid to bound joyfully into heaven when it's our time."

To do or to talk about...

Did you find books about death to read to your child? (See suggestions on page 23.) As Holy Week approaches, you may want to have those books on hand. Don't force the question, but don't be afraid to mention death in front of your children. If they perceive that you're okay talking about death, they will be less likely to treat it as a forbidden subject.

Let us pray...

Lord Jesus,
help us to live each day of this life
so that we are prepared for heaven,
and give us the grace to trust that
all will be well.
We pray, Lord, let us be like you.
Amen.

Wednesday: Fifth Week of Lent

To think about...

There are three things we need to lead a good Christian life, and all three are in the Lazarus story. The first of these is grace. In the story about Lazarus being brought back to life, grace is when Jesus shouts, "Lazarus, come out!" Jesus calls us to come out of the little tombs we find ourselves stuck in. Sometimes it's a tomb of anger, bitterness, or jealousy—and Jesus calls us to forgive, to let go, and to move on. Sometimes it's a tomb of the fear of change, and Jesus calls us to be brave and trust him. Sometimes it a tomb of addiction or bad habits—drinking too much, eating too much, spending too much money, watching too much TV, playing too much with electronic games. Jesus calls us out of that tomb, too, into a full, gracious, beautiful life.

To do or to talk about...

Where do you need grace? What's not working in your family life? Finances? School? Work? A cluttered house that doesn't feel homey? Weight issues? Health issues? Bad habits? Sometimes we think we can only talk to Jesus about the big stuff like world peace. Try bringing even "little problems" to Jesus in prayer. Let everyone in the family say where they really want the grace to get unstuck.

Let us pray...

Lord Jesus,
you called Lazarus out of the tomb into new life.
Please, give us the grace we need
to live life free and happy.
We especially need your help with…
(insert here).
We pray, Lord, let us be like you.
Amen.

Thursday: Fifth Week of Lent

To think about...

The second thing we need to lead a good Christian life is will. Will is when Lazarus responds to Jesus' call—to grace. Have you ever been so exhausted that you said you were "dead tired"? Well, Lazarus was "dead tired." It must have been a terrific act of the will to get up and out of that tomb. It might have been so tempting just to lie there, resting, peaceful, no more cares, no more effort. But Lazarus had a will that responded to the grace of Jesus' call. Whether we are "strong-willed" or a more passive person, we all need to train our wills to be attuned to Jesus' desire for us, to respond to grace.

To do or to talk about...

How do we train our wills to want what Jesus wants? We can start by recognizing our own deepest desires. Our deepest desires are placed in us by God, but sometimes it's hard to get in touch with them. We get distracted by the day-to-day demands of life. Keep working on your "bucket list" and think more about where you need help getting unstuck. Then pray together as a family, asking for a will that responds to Jesus' call.

Let us pray...

Lord Jesus,
just as you called Lazarus from his tomb,
you call us to a free, joyful life with you.
Give us the will to respond to your call.
We pray, Lord, let us be like you.
Amen.

Friday: Fifth Week of Lent

To think about...

Grace and will are two of the three things we need to live a Christian life. What's the third? When Lazarus came out of the tomb, he was still wrapped in the cloths that people in the ancient world used to bind the body—kind of a like a mummy. Jesus had just brought Lazarus back to life so we know he could do anything. But does he zap those binding cloths off of Lazarus? No. Instead he says to the people, "Unbind him and let him go." The third thing we need in this Christian life is a community. Jesus calls us, and that's grace. We respond as best we can, and that's will. But the Christian life is not only between me and Jesus. It's me, Jesus, and the community, the Church, the Body of Christ. We need each other. God made us that way, and Jesus came to reveal that we are here to help each other live our new life.

To do or to talk about...

As this week ends, plan to spend next week—Holy Week—with your community. This will take some preparation, just as if you were going out of town for a few days. Set aside time this weekend to prepare the week's meals, even get homework or office work out of the way. Jesus is calling us to community this week. Let's make the time.

Let us pray...

Lord Jesus,
we thank you for the people you have given us to love.
We thank you for our family, our friends, our neighbors
and our church community.
Help us to love each other
as you loved us.
We pray, Lord, let us be like you.
Amen.

Prayer

Prayer to Our Guardian Angel

On the nightstand in our grandchildren's room is a combination night light and music box with paintings of angels on the lampshade. When the music plays—"Angels, We Have Heard on High"—the shade revolves, creating an image of angels dancing on the ceiling. More than once I've heard our grands drop off to sleep while singing, "Glo-ohhhh-ohhhh-ohhhh-ri-ah, in excelsis deo!"

I hope it helps them feel safe and, when they are older and their sleep is troubled by fears of death and the little deaths that are part of this life, that they remember the angels dancing on their ceiling.

This prayer is one our grandparents and even great-grandparents may have learned. Teach it to your children to conquer nighttime "scary-itis."

Angel of God,
my guardian dear,
to whom God's love commits me here,
ever this day be at my side
to light and guard,
to rule and guide.
Amen.

Fun Page

Word Hook-Up: Test Your Lent Knowledge

Match the words or phrases:

1. Fasting ____
2. Almsgiving ____
3. Prayer ____
4. Lazarus ____
5. Samaria ____
6. Tempter ____
7. Ashes ____
8. Sign of the Cross ____
9. Prayer to Mother of Jesus ____
10. Lord's Prayer ____
11. Act of Contrition ____
12. Martha and Mary ____

A. O my God, I am heartily sorry…
B. In the name of the Father and of the Son…
C. Satan
D. Doing without food or eating less food
E. Brother of Martha and Mary
F. Charity to the poor
G. Hail Mary, full of grace…
H. Northern Palestine
I. Jesus' friends in Bethany
J. Lifting our minds and hearts to God
K. Sign of repentance
L. Our Father, who art in heaven…

Answers on page 2

Holy Week

Palm Sunday Gospel
MATTHEW 21:1–11

Jesus rides a donkey through the streets of Jerusalem as the crowds wave palm branches and shout, "Hosanna to the Son of David! Blessed is the one who comes in the name of the Lord!"

Holy Thursday Gospel
JOHN 13:1–15

Jesus eats his Last Supper with his disciples. During the meal, he kneels before the disciples, one at a time, and washes their feet. He tells them, "As I have done for you, so you should do for each other."

Good Friday Gospel
JOHN 19:1–42

The crowd yells, "Crucify him!" and Pilate condemns Jesus to die. He carries his cross to the place called Golgotha (sometimes called Calvary), where he is crucified along with two others. Jesus dies on the cross, and his friends take down his body and place it in a tomb.

Holy Saturday Gospel
MATTHEW 28:1–10; MARK 16:1–7; LUKE 24:1–12

The women friends of Jesus go early in the morning to the tomb where they had placed his body, and they find the tomb empty. They run and tell the other disciples, and all of them are confused and afraid because they don't yet understand that Jesus will rise from the dead.

Palm/Passion Sunday

To think about...

At our parish on Palm Sunday, we begin the Mass outside and process into church as everyone waves palm branches and the choir leads us in singing, "Hosanna to the Son of David." It's always a bit chaotic as people try to walk and sing and keep track of their kids and then find a seat. Maybe because of the chaos, it feels like a happy occasion, even though we know that the same crowd of people who yelled, "Hosanna!" will, in just a few days, yell, "Crucify him!" It's human nature to go along with the crowd. That's why it's important to hang out with the right crowd in the right situations and teach our children to do the same. There's a crowd of people gathering this week. All over the world, Christians are coming together to celebrate Holy Week. This is one time it's a good idea to "join the crowd."

To do and to talk about...

Today plan your week carefully. There are very special church services on Thursday, Friday, Saturday, and Sunday. This week is like a retreat, and it's best if a lot of the practical details are out of the way. So prepare the clothing and meals you'll need for the week and even get a head start on planning your Easter celebration. Consider inviting someone who might be alone for dinner on Holy Thursday or Easter Sunday.

Let us pray...

Lord Jesus,
help us to be faithful in our love for you
and constant in our relationships with others.
We pray, Lord, let us be like you.
Amen.

Monday of Holy Week

To think about...

We live on a small farm with plenty of room for kids to run around, so we're usually the hosts for the family gatherings. On Easter we have a big Easter Egg hunt. I hide plastic eggs, used every year, and put a number in each one. After the hunt, I bring out a large basket filled with numbered prizes—packages of jelly beans, chocolate bunnies, art supplies, little toys for the kids, and one year a pineapple that was a big hit. Many of the prizes have notes attached directing the prizewinner to do something: "Lead the group in the bunny hop." "Trade prizes with someone, but don't make anyone cry." (This after a five-year-old lost her favorite prize.) "Act out a charade of 'The Greatest Story Ever Told.'" The last prizewinner always has to direct the rest of us as we sing along with a recording of the "Hallelujah Chorus."

To do and to talk about...

How do you celebrate Easter? Continue preparing the clothes and meals and other practical details for the rest of this week, including your Easter celebration. Don't forget to invite someone who might otherwise be alone on Holy Thursday or Easter Sunday. Today or tomorrow, you may also want to pray the Stations of the Cross or, if you haven't already, go to confession.

Let us pray...

Lord Jesus,
the egg is a symbol of new life
and in you we have the promise of life everlasting.
Help us to believe in your promises.
We pray, Lord, let us be like you.
Amen.

Tuesday of Holy Week

To think about...

I didn't discover the Church until I was twenty-one years old. Raised without Christian faith, I was excited by what I found and, with only two weeks of instruction, accepted baptism from a charismatic Jesuit priest. (There was no RCIA in those days.) As you can imagine, I was a pretty green Catholic. Several weeks after I was baptized, I saw in the church bulletin an announcement of the Triduum schedule. As I discovered later, Triduum just means "three days." The Easter Triduum begins with the Holy Thursday evening Mass of the Lord's Supper and ends at sundown on Easter Sunday. I showed up at church on Holy Thursday night, and the priest whispered to me, "Just do what everyone else does." I was very moved by everything I saw and heard and smelled during those days. I think those who pay very close attention during the Triduum celebrations can learn almost all they need to know about being a follower of Jesus.

To do and to talk about...

Continue with your Easter preparations so that you can fully participate in the Triduum celebrations. Do you make Easter baskets for each child? Buy something new to wear to Easter Sunday Mass? Shop for special foods for the Easter dinner? When you're out shopping, buy a white or light colored pillar candle—the tallest one you can find—and some whole cloves. We'll talk about what to do with those later.

Let us pray...

Lord Jesus,
help us get ready for Easter so that we can set aside
our busyness and celebrate the Triduum as a family.
May we grow closer to you and to all those who love you.
We pray, Lord, let us be like you.
Amen.

Wednesday of Holy Week

To think about...

Sometimes today is called "Spy Wednesday" because Judas is getting ready to betray Jesus. Why do good people do bad things? Most of the folks yelling, "Crucify him!" were probably not bad people. Saint Peter was a good man and Jesus' choice for leading the church, and yet he behaved like a coward and denied Jesus. And it seems that Judas was a bad man, but in the end, he was sad about betraying Jesus. We might think we'd never deny Jesus or betray him, but if we have ever failed to defend someone when they were being teased or treated unjustly, if we've ever betrayed someone by talking badly about them or breaking a promise to them, then we know how easy it is to do bad things.

To do and to talk about...

There are a lot of sinful influences in our world—influences that may lead us or our children to do what we don't want to do. Belonging to a church community can help keep us and our children on the path with Jesus. Do whatever you need to do today so that the whole family can join your church community at the Triduum celebrations starting tomorrow night. Count up the money in your alms vessel to give to the poor. We put ours in the Holy Thursday collection which, in our parish, is always for our food pantry. Decide who will receive your offering and pick a time to take the money to them.

Let us pray...

Lord Jesus,
we are sorry for the times when we have failed
to stand up for others or betrayed those who trusted us.
Please forgive us.
We pray, Lord, help us to be like you.
Amen.

Holy Thursday

To think about...

Tonight is the celebration of the Mass of the Lord's Supper. Go and take your children. Notice that the purple of Lent is gone, and there is a white cloth and flowers on the altar. At the beginning, you will sing the Gloria, announcing the end of Lent and the beginning of the Triduum. After the homily, the priest will wash the feet of some parishioners. See how humble the priest looks kneeling there, and remember that Jesus did the same thing; that this is a symbol of Christian leadership, the leadership of a servant. After Holy Communion, there may be a procession with the Eucharist to an Altar of Repose. This is an ancient custom when all the eucharistic bread is removed from the church, and the vigil light is extinguished in preparation for the solemn service tomorrow remembering our Lord's passion and death. I always think of our middle son when he was just five years old, who, at this point in the service, whispered to his godmother, "I feel like all the love has gone out of my heart."

To do and to talk about...

Have dinner together tonight and, even if it's just sandwiches or pizza, put a cloth and flowers on the table. Place your most beautiful bowl of water on the table and wash each other's hands and dry them carefully with a clean cloth. Tell your children that's what the priest will do tonight to some people's feet. Be sure and say grace before you eat.

Let us pray...

Come, Lord Jesus, be our guest and let these gifts
to us be blessed. And Lord we pray, especially on this
night when we remember your Last Supper,
Lord, let us be like you.
Amen.

Good Friday

To think about...

Today's service is called the Celebration of the Lord's Passion. The solemnity and the prayerfulness of the community will impress even little children. After the readings, including Saint John's account of the crucifixion of Jesus, a cross will be displayed for everyone to venerate—to honor. You may venerate the cross by bowing, genuflecting, kissing, or touching it reverently. Everyone venerates the cross—sinners and near saints, old and young, rich and poor. The cross is one thing we all have in common. We all suffer. We all lose people we love. We all die.

To do and to talk about...

Even very little children are aware of death and have questions. Don't evade these questions. Let your children express their concerns and answer them truthfully. Perhaps read to your children one of your books about death (see page 23), and tonight, remember in prayer anyone who has died among your loved ones, including pets. (Today is a fast day. See the rules for fasting on page 8.)

Let us pray...

Lord Jesus,
we thank you for dying for us
and for making death a beginning
of new life in heaven with you.
Bless those we love who have died (names)
and tell them we love them.
We pray, Lord, let us be like you.
Amen.

Holy Saturday

To think about...

One year after the Easter Vigil, a parishioner told me how sad he was because for seventy years of Catholic life, he had never been to the Vigil and only came that year because he was asked to be a sponsor of someone who was baptized. He said he would never miss again. Yes, the Easter Vigil is long—at least longer than the average Sunday Mass—and maybe too long for little children. When my children were very young, we took them dressed in their pajamas to the first part of the service—the Service of Light. Standing in the dark church lit only by the candles held by everyone present and listening to the sung Easter Proclamation impresses even very little children. If they're restless, take them home before the Liturgy of the Word begins. After we hear from the prophets of the Old Testament, we sing, for the first time since Lent began, "Alleluia!" to herald the Gospel of the resurrection. If your children are still awake, stay for the baptism and reception of new members of the church, and by then, you're almost home.

To do and to talk about...

Sometime today find the candle and cloves you bought and create an Easter candle for your home. Decorate it with five whole cloves, representing the wounds of Christ, in the form of a cross. When you pray before supper tonight, trace the cross on the candle and say the prayer below. Be sure to get a nap today and eat a good dinner. Then go to church.

Let us pray...

By his wounds, holy and glorious,
may he protect and preserve us
who is Christ the Lord.
We pray, Lord, let us be like you.
Amen.

Prayer

Apostles' Creed

I direct a group we call the Combined Christian Choir—over one hundred singers from all the Christian congregations in our town. One thing we have in common is The Apostles' Creed, so called because it is considered to be a true summary of the faith of the original Apostles. We sing an arrangement of this creed that is so rollicking and upbeat that it's hard to believe the text dates back so many centuries.

This is not the Creed we proclaim at Mass—that's the Nicene Creed, dating to the Council of Nicaea in 325. The Apostles' Creed is part of the prayer of the rosary. It's good to memorize them both (although I confess I get easily derailed from one to the other). Proclaim the creed as a joyous expression of our faith, all made possible by the events we remember and celebrate this week.

I believe in God, the Father almighty,
Creator of heaven and earth,
and in Jesus Christ, his only Son,
our Lord, who was conceived
by the Holy Spirit, born of the Virgin Mary,
suffered under Pontius Pilate,
was crucified, died and was buried;
He descended into hell; on the third day he rose again
from the dead; he ascended into heaven,
and is seated at the right hand
of God the Father almighty;
from there he will come to judge the living and the dead.
I believe in the Holy Spirit, the holy catholic Church,
the communion of saints, the forgiveness of sins,
the resurrection of the body, and life everlasting.
Amen.

Scrambled Words or Scrambled Eggs?

It's almost time to hunt for Easter eggs. For now, have fun hunting for the right word.

TASREE _____

GEG _____

HOOCCALTE _____

BELLJYNEAS _____

NYBUN _____

TESKAB _____

TONBEN _____

SESJU _____

THUN _____

LIALEALU _____

YLLI _____

ENSIR _____

Answers on page 2

Easter Sunday

Early on the first day of the week, while it was still dark, Mary Magdalene came to the tomb and saw that the stone had been removed from the tomb. So she ran and went to Simon Peter and the other disciple, the one whom Jesus loved, and said to them, "They have taken the Lord out of the tomb, and we do not know where they have laid him." Then Peter and the other disciple set out and went toward the tomb. The two were running together, but the other disciple outran Peter and reached the tomb first. He bent down to look in and saw the linen wrappings lying there, but he did not go in. Then Simon Peter came, following him, and went into the tomb. He saw the linen wrappings lying there, and the cloth that had been on Jesus' head, not lying with the linen wrappings but rolled up in a place by itself. Then the other disciple, who reached the tomb first, also went in, and he saw and believed; for as yet they did not understand the scripture, that he must rise from the dead.

Come Holy Spirit

I remember well my first Easter as a Catholic. After a very rich Lent and Holy Week, I left Mass that Easter morning feeling kind of let down and asking myself, "Well, Jesus is risen, but what about me?" I suppose that's how the first disciples felt—left alone and confused after the daily company of their friend and teacher, Jesus.

Easter can bring a kind of relief—we get to eat chocolate again!— but it can also be disappointing to leave this time of spiritual renewal. What I discovered after my first Easter Sunday is that the Easter season lasts fifty days and culminates with the Feast of Pentecost, the celebration of the sending of the Holy Spirit. Memorize this prayer to the Holy Spirit and pray it throughout this season. You may want to let different family members take turns being the Leader. Don't forget to light your Easter candle.

Leader *Come, Holy Spirit, fill the hearts of your faithful*

All **and enkindle in them the fire of your love.**

Leader *Send forth your Spirit, and they shall be created*

All **and you shall renew the face of the earth.**

Leader *Let us pray...*

All **O God, who has taught the hearts of the faithful by the light of the Holy Spirit, grant that by the gift of the same Spirit we may be always truly wise and ever rejoice in his consolation, through Christ our Lord.**

Amen.

Fun Page

Color by Number: Create Glorious Color

Have you ever seen the *Wizard of Oz*? When Dorothy is in Kansas, the picture is in black and white, but as soon as she arrives in Oz, we see glorious color! That's what it's like when we understand that Jesus is risen from the dead. Instead of living our lives in black and white, all around seems brighter and full of life. Now you get to add the only color to this little book.

1. Yellow
2. Red
3. Blue
4. Green
5. Orange
6. Purple